About the Author

With an M.Sc. in Educational Psychology, a B.A (hons) and a B.Ed., Lesley Kahney worked as a teacher, educational psychologist and finally as a manager of an Early Years Inclusion Service.

Now retired, she often visits the Isle of Skye from her home in Milton Keynes, to do volunteer work and to find inspiration for her poetry and painting.

She enjoys country walks, art, music, literature and Buddhism. She has a son who is a musician.

Dedication

To
my son Acle Kahney,
to Ed Luke, where my poetry journey began,
and wildlife lovers everywhere.

To Hugh,
with warm wishes
& happy memories,
Lesley x

Lesley Kahney

A Spoondrift of Pearls

Austin Macauley Publishers™

LONDON • CAMBRIDGE • NEW YORK • SHARJAH

A CIP catalogue record for this title is available from the British Library.

ISBN 9781528982788 (Paperback)
ISBN 9781528982795 (ePub e-book)

www.austinmacauley.com

First Published (2020)
Austin Macauley Publishers Ltd
25 Canada Square
Canary Wharf
London
E14 5LQ

Acknowledgements

I am grateful to
the kind permission of:
The Gavin Maxwell Enterprises Estate c/o The Marsh Agency
Ltd.,
and Virginia McKenna,
without whose love for Gavin Maxwell and Eilean Bàn, this book
would not have been written.

I also give thanks to:
the Bright Water Trust for giving me the opportunity to serve as
volunteer warden on the island of Eilean Bàn,
John for his enduring support,
David MacLennan and Sam Young for their encouragement,
and Austin Macauley Publishers.

A Spoondrift of Pearls is a collection of poems inspired by the tiny four-acre island, Eilean Bàn, lying between the mainland of Scotland and the Misty Isle of Skye.

It was home to Gavin Maxwell for the last eighteen months of his life, before his death on 7th September 1969. Gavin was famous for his book *Ring of Bright Water*, but he had many talents, including artist, poet, traveller, naturalist, businessman, visionary and writer.

The tiny, magical island is still home to a lighthouse, the lighthouse keeper's cottages, seals and otters. I had the privilege to work there for eight to nine months over a period of three years, as volunteer warden for the Bright Water Trust.

These poems are for anyone who finds pleasure in nature.

Contents

Island Dawn

Dew dank, quartz coals
spit life into smouldering clouds,
stoking wakening warmth.

Whirring curlew wings
send smoke signals
to violet skies.

On resting pebbles,
the sea breathes
like blacksmith bellows.

A single cormorant
knowing it has all day,
dives slowly,
slicing waves with a
sword forged by light.

Stars disappear.
The spark catches, burns,
evaporating a world in the dew.
Night is vanquished
and hope finds you.

Island Edge

An east wind calls.
Irritated,
waves listen and prickle.
Black, they agitate
a revolution
going nowhere.

Stable wind transforms.
With old smokers' voices,
seagulls circle and cry,
"See. It's easy.
Just fly."

A Mother's Lament

A growling grey slate sky.
Reverberating stillness.
A burbling murmuring
rises and falls gently
trickling up from the gorse,
evocative of mosses
and faint mists shrouding marshes,
a sad forlorn hopeless call.

The female cuckoo laments
to an iron moon and
pulls down the clouds
to blanket her baby lost,
in another's nest.

Milky Way

With the out breath of a resting cat
night apathetically wrestles day.
Stars salt the sky, spilt on the robe
spreading behind the Milky Way.

Air sharp as needles stitch the wound
of a bleeding mountain stream
and strokes to sleep a cottage door
under a flickering lighthouse beam.

Sea pulls and strains to unglue rocks;
breathing hard the waves at war,
surrender with a cough of spray
on the darkening island shore.

A trawler engine heartbeat throbs,
mobbed by seagull mafia,
shaking down the vaulted waves
guarding river's silver.

In times of dark the lost stay lost.
The star robe shrugs and sighs.
The traveller is reconciled
to moments fleeting by.

Seals

Enduring rocks
meet the sky
where yellow light
cradles unforgiving laps
to raging births.

Red flotsam afterbirth
waits like wounds
torn by gulls
pecking at
forgotten hurts.

The sea bleeds
her true rawness
while light
wraps a bandage
tied by matron winds.

The mother's nose
draws down
fingers of ointment,
to her new-born pup,
nudging him to the rock's end.

Squabbling seagulls sink.
Antiseptic sun
evaporates
and sea celebrates
birth, euphoric.

Isle of Soay

… a streak -
gun silver harpoon whistles,

rending air and sea and flesh,
penetrating her distress.

Thunderous spray leaps,
showering all with bleeding sparks.

Shark, basking gently,
opens up her heart, to commune,

a love song to the ocean,
mingling with brine.

The fisherman saw her eye
step into the hunter's moon,

a knowing exchanged embrace,
a mother's sacrifice.

His dispassion curdled -
as he opened up his heart to her death.

Fairy Pools

Birthed from Hades, cursing, crawling
over Mother Nature's lap;
fleeing onwards, spewing spoondrift,
leaping crags and iron land.

River throws her head back laughing,
showing throat of forest glass,
calling all to dive into her
frosted caves of icy blast.

Eyes of mullion showing panic,
heartbeat throbbing from the race,
gasping, feeling, it's too late -
to escape the devil's face.

Daughter dervish missionary,
shouts the message of the night,
fingers reaching under stones,
pulls and tears the wings off sprites.

No-one hears it, no-one cares,
tiny screams towards the moon.
Fairy realm obliterated
in cascading fairy pools.

Winter Island

Now is the dark shrunk fast,
around the wintering heart.
Cold treacle pewter flows
with madness over rocks.

A headache watches slowly,
a body racked, betrayed.
Pine marten crouches, waits,
heart sore for small crushed lives.

The wounds cannot be seen,
they shrivelled long ago.
The home is in the cut,
a cradle for his soul.

Skies brutal wink impassive,
his pale face freezes low
and stars shrink shyly back,
breathing hysteria black.

Heart-shaped Lock

Tender dark reminder of
oyster catcher wing beats,

a lover's kiss of waves
pushing passionately
at lungs' resistant locks,
coaxing them to open.

Rushing for union
water mingles with blood and bone,
bursting the heart,
returning to life's home.

A violent marriage of air
and water, tyrannical death
pebbles the marriage bed,
seaweed a funeral shroud.

Now a heart-shaped lock
clings to life and says,
"This soft heart shut"
and the iron hardness mocks -

"he went and drowned".
Life's hair and skin and bone,
all heart's ease just bloody gone,
wed to a metal bridge.

Your eyes close remembering -
the sound of tender life beat over.

Nocturne

Indigo seas, indigo trees, old fishing boats,
where do the trawlers go
steaming through snow?

Fastened up gates, fastened up doors, white frosty trees,
truculent waves smelling of peat,
jostling their dreams.

Freezing dark air, freezing dark breath, frozen black strait,
loud haunted seagulls chasing their fate:
shadows on ripples, souls hid from hate.

Pale light moon, pale light path, yellow lighthouse,
stars open in waves, screaming out,
"Faith".

Blue

Blue draws back the curtains of night's hold.

Quartz crumbles, hurling up white banners -
      cutting ribbons to the day.

Greylags soar. Haunting calls float.

Feathers frail take note of wings whirring -
      and his voice calling.

Settling on sapphire, they sing softly to a spoondrift of pearls.

Ribbons of cloud connect to the man long gone.

Sea breathes. Blue.
      Only the waves go on calling and calling.

Lighthouse

Waves suck in their breath.
The sea, stained by doubt,
shuffles from the shore.

The moon cross examines
the taciturn lighthouse.
Wrenched from rocks, it vows

to stones asleep,
snoring in their dreams,
elusive in denial.

Curlews call,
casting a beam
in recesses of minds.

The jewels of night
soften and shine
their kindness.

The tower shakes,
waking sea bed judges
and memories rush, releasing

forgiveness, floating on the foam.

In the Midnight Moment

In this midnight moment
measuring time by stars,
a ripple speaks momentously
though dinghies nod at nothing.

I give you the sound that
from the mystery grows,
sea pinks and tiny voles
and moist air dropping down.

The message from the sea hosts
sounds of droplets sparkling,
grumbling pebbles rolling
and soaring gulls in freedom.

Listen to the echo
that from your heart grows out -
seeds settling in the mind,
finding alchemy in now.

In this midnight moment -
all life's reveries are true -

stars, woman, seas and shrews -
I'd give you this moon.

Waiting

Narrating seagulls over cottage rooftop,
chattering about the bread they dropped,
settle and sit patiently looking out to sea,
content to rest and be.

The visitor looks along the island trail
waiting for his old late friend.
He sits and stares, surveying -
astounded by the wren.

Twisted, pinned, preserved,
the trees no longer wait;
busy, their flexible curve
the very nerve of rocks and wind.

The rocks all know the meaning,
of watching lichens spreading,
whilst the moon bends the sea
into energy rolling.

Now you wait for his waiting.
Watching his pain.

You did that once before -
choosing to persevere, unsure.
Will you cry at the leaving of the gulls,
at the absurdity of love that shrugs?

This island guards its loss.
It rends the winds and sends
a message to the shore -
a correspondence with the otters, waiting.

The visitor turned to his friend,
aching,
and they went in to cut the bread
for tea.

White Island Cottage

Sulking stones,
mouldy with constant battering
and chastisement from the sea,
glare at the frowning skyline.

Lighthouse keepers feel
the frozen sea gods close.
They stamp their feet,
blow on their hands
and light their lamps.

Rain bodies tumble down -
droplet icy fireflies
dancing in the lamplight,
chafing at their faces
braving wild weather.

Viking ghosts cleaved in cliffs
sever from their sleep
to call infatuated souls.

Black arms of waves stretch out
to take their toll
on the man who touched the taste
of freedom and gave his soul.

The sun's pale head
sinks heavy like lead
and darkness shrouds

these families cowed
hiding from the storm,
listening to the clash of Viking swords.

Some locals know they march
but others say they echo
from off the island's cliffs.

We search this island's secrets -
its stones and waves and home,
to find otter eyes that stare
at treacherous stars at prayer.

All on an island worn and pure,
          in this cottage, white and sure.

Teko

Once his heart was
cast in volcanic love,

delving oceans deep,
sleeping in the wedge of the wind.

Now alone in the black of space,
at the primitive pine's end,

bursting with the fire of passion
where traces of smoke hang,

the flames of dawn look on,
breathing life into tired lungs.

It is enough. Stars steal his breath
as he swims the depth of bright seas.

Elgol

Battering winds bruise purple moors,
softened
by endless skies.

Grey dampness hangs like a cloak,
comforting
trees scanned by eagles.

Mutated daisies labour for air,
gasping
and are exceptional.

Broods of boats nod their dissent,
safe
in cauldron's arms.

Bees' honeycomb hardens into quartz,
forming
unnatural cliffs.

A harsh and independent place,
cruel
but protective.

Boats sputter a furrow to where you are,
impermanent
with all that is.

Meditation

When you sit in stillness
breath floats across the years
whispering of ancestors
and moments trapped in tar.

Hope retreats
from plumbing vision's depths,
that nettle bed of dreams -
a smoke cloud.

Bird song fades,
scratching your throat,
you struggle to hold
this diving in caves.

Fingers swell like balloons
and body parts swim apart,
leaving soon a gaping space
in place of your heart.

Yesterday's bubble
wafts upwards on a breeze
levelling out stubble,
squeezing ocean's ripples.

The river's breath
flows over your head.
Blackness swirls and swallows you
and stars spit out your toes.

Flower Moon

Ghost like and lacking effort, Flower Moon rises pale,
   inhaling May time blooms.

Clouds too lazy to exhale, collapse on the horizon.
   Streetlights twinkle, deafening.

Sun droops, exhausted, catching the windows
   a glancing blow of orange brilliance, then dumb.

The blackbird sings a vesper at the sun's evensong,
   a prehistoric prayer in trees on Mesozoic rocks.

The notes warble, then blind.

Doors sleep, window lids flutter.
   United in our search for sleep,

   we disappear.

Trumpan

In shadows, slender necks nod,
    holding private conversations -
        their business — scent of salt and ferns,

unconcerned with mountains levitating
    over ice blue waters
        or the meditating seas confusing light and miraged skies.

Standing still you see the primrose government
    and hear the cuckoo's call.
        Invisible skylark expands your heart.

You feel the thread,
    its tendrel part
        and wonder at the path you followed here.

You turn to listen and you know,
    this moment is enough.

South West Wind

The south west wind argued with the walls,
shouting unclearly, brawling
and flinging aimless pellets of rain
like a mad man beyond the pale.

Re-gathering strength to chew at the corners of the house,
shouting and slicing at the belly of the clouds,
the wind pirouetted a fandango of rain and gusts -
blustering in red shoes through the night.

In the exhausted morning cadence,
new sober ferns shook and glistened.
Light, with the vividness of a woodcutter's blade,
shone a spotlight on prisms,

and in the shadows, a robin stepped forward -
                singing.

Alone

Yesterday,
the east wind ran off,
deserting the sun to
push through clouds alone.
It takes effort to ease
sheep into the fold.

The cold wind gone,
the sheep graze in drifts,
the sun winds up
mechanical birds
singing reiteratively.

Nothing artificial about
their intelligence, their
desire to be alive
evident in every note.

An Interruption

A shadow

sliced the conversation
beating black at glass, bright.

With consternation we agitated

like moths to light.

Circling round the flailing feathers,
my hands joined the tiniest lightness -

seed weight of feather, heart and bone,
with blue, the deepest, iridescent hue.

We breathed as the world paused

Shh!! Shh!!

I knew
the swallow's eye sought mine
an age in this moment of time - eternity!

A long tail. A flash of red.
It soared from me

and was free.

The Long Room

Do you remember who lived here -
the island with its heather,
wound of a bridge
and lighthouse, a long time dark,

empty now,

on the edge of a sea shoving its
way around the sound,
the stark house welded to a mound
of rocks with twisted rowan trees,

full of musty memories?

Now people come and visit here.
Two old ladies come back each year.
Summer last, she crept reluctant
to scatter the ashes of her husband,
to mingle with the otter atoms.

Back then there was purpose and parties.

Today they left,
leaving phantoms
but taking all our husbands with them.

Now it's still, almost condemned,

but the empty hearths in the Long Room,
are smoke blackened by the evidence of warmth.

Turn to the south and remember them,
and think of him.

Then.

Bluebells

This is the time of bluebell spires
                rising up from ravaged,
                        windswept hillsides.

Blue and lilac silent peals
                reveal their secret of renewal.
                        Democracy gives each a voice.

"This is our time, our moment
                of perfumed beauty,
                        of calling earth to action.

A time to heal the scars,
                if it's not too late to hear -
                        our far away bells ringing."

Lost

Lost and wandering in the wasteland,
staring at ink skies,
where stars have disappeared,
        you know how sadness feels.

There is no escape from this grief
        that tugs at your knees.

Stepping over fallen trees
and wading through windswept waves,
vanishing into the darkness,
        you know this path is yours.

In the first streaks of dawn
seagulls will cry out
and rise high upon the wind,
        circling and calling you to them.

Stars will twinkle and drop their forgiveness.
Winds will pluck at you and remind you,

that your pain is your connection,
        to all you love and your life.

Otter

With voices hushed we crept between the sheep
and in the grass and sand in late sun's rays,
we sat down close to watch and vigil keep.

Across the wrinkled waves we held our gaze -
with gleam of pink and fading violet glow,
the ripples parted to reveal a head.

We glimpsed in joy before it went below
to leave a trail, a fragile silver thread.
Again, a sudden solitary shape!

The waves revealed an agile sleek-lined body,
shining in the gentle glass seascape
that twinkled in the purple bright aurora.

In awe we sat to watch the flowing otter,
fishing, diving deeper for an augur.

The Bothy

Hewn, irregular steps,
climb to the bothy,
like they were made for a drunken giant,
wet and lichen covered, defiant,
     with no regard for hold of foot.

Ferns droop down, stooped
by the weight of rain drops,
bowing to unseen royalty,
dragging their caps in the ground,
     beseeching in their frailty.

I open the door to darkness,
the light and sound of the sea behind me,
     no wild cat cry,
     washer woman nod
     or shepherd's smile to greet me -

only its silence and musty smell -
     consenting.

A million secrets to tell,
stretching back
     and dwelling in its scent.

Twilight

Twilight draws her cloak across the day
shielding tardy pink and golden glows.

Nine o'clock.

Violet falling, evening comes to stay.
Air and water hushed and silent grows,

lighting gold.

Seagulls circle round the darkened bay
crying for the peaceful end of day.

Here we stay.

Water chill and grey, with pink soft ripples,
loafs and notes the skimming seagulls'

squawking calls.

In the dimming harbour a grey seal
stares with intense eyes and tells us heal.

Writing

Running through the grass the mouse scribbles
her name in tiny letters, lines joined together.
Hopping cockily the robin points to his initials
on the path. The spider weaves another
secret message that only flies can read.

Tiny calligraphic marks eaten by a caterpillar
suggest an enigmatic letter.
Otter parts the waves to reveal a letter v.
Swans look down as they leave brush marks in the sky,
each looking to the other for a written reply.

Hieroglyphics are left by the patterns of seeds,
blown into patterns by a passing breeze.
Greylags fly beating patterns high, searching
for the man that called them, burning
to see them; urging them to land.

A flow of ripples paints a picture, in the sand,
a lecture left by seals. Cormorants dive
a full stop and the man who's died -
sits - still at his desk and writes.
All leave their mark, each with their own device.

Author

The island holds art at its edges.
Oyster catchers make their nest
and lay their eggs, creating.
Music flows as evening falls
from composer curlews.

Otter writes poetry in the waves,
with ambiguous and fluid phrase.
Daily news is squawked by seagulls who,
are the ocean's journalists.

Eel scribblers and note-taking divers
are unaware of ghost writers
hiding in the walls.

Author sits at his desk to pour his tales
and we feel all that remains.

Hunter

Pumpkin coloured Hunter's Moon, large and bright
lends his magic to the night. Otter glides
in evening light, conjuring plans and skills.

Stealth like huntsman hides to pounce, focused face
unseen by exposed mouse. Seagull scavengers
filch the eggs, laid by fellow travellers.

Night-time badgers cast their spells deep in clay.
Questing wizard plummets down, lord of moving prey.
Mobbed by trickster crows, talons take their prize.

Alchemy creeps where innocence thrives.
Man hunts them all by light of sun or moon
and death comes quick from his harpoon.

Rowan Tree

On a hillside in the depth of night,
alarmed gorse plucks her dress.
Stumbling, arms wrap around the tree,
tumbling secrets in pouring rain,
confessing curses in passionate pain.

Blood red berries drop their grace.
Heavy secrets lace the tree,
parchment white, like old man's beard.
The old omerta creases limbs,
betrayals shouldered, too much to bear.

Seeking comfort, on she goes.
Time releases consequence.
Truth unfolds, leaving tears on stones.
Truth obsessed, burdened tree,
remorseful, stands no longer.

Harvest Moon

An egg yolk balances,
ruptures open
and dribbles a citrine tail
from the dark hilltop farm,
pouring plumage on the spume;
the light a nativity of gold.

Waves peck at the shore edge,
foraging for kernels of beams.
Preening themselves and muttering,
the waves nest and perch
against cold rocks, ruffling their spray,
settling for calm.

Golden harvest over,
low stubble waves grow pale.
Gamekeeper whistles to his chicks -
soothing their constant nibbling,
hiding the looming harm,
knowing the season's
open.

Raven Seek Thy Brother

Like falling out of bed -
          two fell from a tree,
noisily above the wind,
stark against the sterling sea.

Silver pierced black eyes,
oily wings, petrol blue shaman cloaks,
slithered through the sky,
tumbling and rising,
chasing bitter spells.

Trees fidgeted with arcane tales to tell,
a moving web of bones,
holding a nest of skulls,
with goblets of mouse blood.

The ravens navigated
their course, oblivious,
automatic in their skill.

One took roost in the ash tree
and surveyed the misty hill,
prophesying death and calling all -
          rabbit, mouse and owl.

A hint of Morrighan's cloak
in the corner of his eye,
a deception of death,
an unkindness of ravens,

alone, he called his brother
falling to the sea ...

        "Raven seek thy brother".

Fern City

Sat in these ferns,
sap green, stained-glass windows
willow light in a shape shifting church.

Beyond kaleidoscopic arches,
a perfect city rises for summer dwelling -
frond pillows, robes, parasols and palaces.

Shepherd sun relaxes,
pipits parachute, compelling leaves to unfrock
and summer passes.

Crawling through stem pillars, in dark naves,
beating bracken's crumbling, smoking ashes,
breathing in the earthy scent of spores,

we read the changes like a clock.
The coming bracken - end of childhood,
leaving cremated ferns to earth returned.

Island Trust

I carry this island with me,
not heavy in a bag
but light as mists, settled like a shroud,
obscuring sight and sound.

I see this island in me, with
parting mists and rainbows -
seagulls that fall and resurrect
on winds that tease and rip.

I hear this island - rattling pebbles,
groaning waves, creating peril,
Cailleach shaking twisted trees,
in moonlight's shadows, wailing.

I feel this island burning
bright by day and in my heart,
with selkies birthing
pups on sun-scorched rocks.

I taste the salt
that to the pebbles clings,
in desperate bids to halt
the dogged tidal waves.

I smell the musty mould of age,
in pages turned within the room -
this glorious stage, your home,
that sits and waits for you.

I know the morning birds that celebrate,
the simple sunshine, seeds,
the rising mists, reclining warmth,
the mystery and hope.

I carry this island to you.
I entrust you this island -
expansive, wild and free.

When You Sleep on the Island

When you sleep on the island
thick cottage walls embrace you
and the sage green lichen that grew
on the water tank by the door
becomes a blanket for
small insects and flies
that sleep and you feel
the island like a band flowing
out from your heart. You extend
through walls to fall to your knees
in the grass and you feel the tiny
berries and pimpernels mending
your heart, blood red and shiny,
with tiny stitches of silver moonlight
marrying with the thread wound round
the surgery opening you to the sensation,
that the sea is a distant conversation,
irrelevant yet secure
because this is your
conversation with yourself,
with the earth,
your birth, this is your
place, safe, a place for everyman
and woman.

Fire

A hard time he had of it -
recovering from the fire,
balancing his heart and mind.

Montbretia on the path
burns with its own fire,
a warmth of welcome,
hinting at the flames
that claimed his home.
Those dreadful words of 'Fire! Fire!',
the rushing, frantic searching
in the purging fire,
when Robert Frost's ice
would certainly have sufficed,
at the coldest time of year.
Here, in the fired home
one otter drowned in flames,
burnt through till
stars peeped out in the gloaming
and all was lost, smouldering.

The long room has two hearths
for roaring flames,
that Aristotle element,
stoked by homely thoughts,
caught and kept by cosy dogs,
sleeping lazily by both hearths,
wooden shutters closed
keeping winds' angry proposals
out and undisclosed.

The grates are empty now.
Cold and stone grey
ashes denoting that once
the flames burnt bright,
that he sat visualising his own tigers,
dreaming till the embers burnt white.

Fire lit his soul.
His spirit was his sail to far flung places.
He tempered reason and passion
and gave nature credence
till his soul rose like a phoenix from the ashes.

Island Heart

I lay this island in your hand,
whose shores held by the wind
whisper in ears of rocks,
tearing a smile.

Turn it round to see trawlers
taking satisfaction
of returning from the broken ribs of waves
to yellow warmth of home.

Lift the island to your ear.
Hear it call the songs of shells
and turquoise mermaids
swimming with the sound of sea bells,

ripping memories of the ancients
from the sky that blankets all,
uniting earth and sky and sea
as everything and nothing.

If you stumble from your fear
that rattles at your back,
embrace the sea, the salt and sand
and know the stillness that's in nothing.

Sit to see the stars leap in your lap,
all snapped from wishes in the waves,
connected to the map
of your distant childhood.

You will feel the edges of the island
tearing you and holding you -
a snare's trap of fur and tooth
binding your heart.

Imprinted with ghosts,
skulking uncertain,
otters and selkies tread lightly
through fern and moss and dew,

kissing fish that are afraid.

Oyster Catchers

We shriek above the rocks,
the shrillness ripped from our throats.
We know it's futile, but still we swoop and hope.

Gull! Gull!

They scream food,
their huge wings casting shadows over our shallow nest,
scraped in a clump of sea pinks clutching rocks.

Egg! Egg!

No babe to wander sea torn skies
or moult to priestly robes.

Gone! Gone!

We peck and displace our pain,
muttering and wailing
demented ghosts falling from the rocks.

Stoic! Stoic!

Paired, steadfast, romantic,
we face another year gone.

Another year with no young to carry on.

Independence

Searching, the wind misses the door,
and knocks around the back.

"Come in. No use whistling in confusion
like a drunk man trying the lock."

Shaking the handle with angry intent,
the wind continues its fight,

shouting as the one with the only right,
with no insight into why it was sent.

The mist, lying lethargic on the loch
is roused from laziness by the wind's knock

and with a glance over its shoulder starts to tip toe off.
The clouds, all of a blather, catch the wind's drift,

and furrow through waves like a paddle steamer,
trailing exhausted stars until dawn.

The moon on the water observes
and indicates the moment to go - to independence.

No sudden, ripped departure, but a gradual moving on.

The Path

Enter through the wooden gate,
    where mystery hangs like a dew-drop necklace.
The journey that brought you here remains
a part of the voyage ahead.
The invitation of the path chains you:
to frame what sustains you.

This path, overhung with birch,
hears when you approach.
The birds reproach your interruption,
punctuating their conversations,
then leave you in welcome seclusion.

You listen to the path speaking
in the tangled undergrowth that loiters -
this giant cave to fuzzy shrews
shooting faster than running spiders.
Thoughts unravel absorbing
the island that transforms.

Striding through dark tunnels
of rowans and montbretia,
slight candles smoulder lower
in the gloomy jungle
of shrines to tombs and skulls,
and you want to stay with Teko's stone

but months from now you'll feel the island's pull
of otters, mountains, life.
Close the gate and the path continues.
There's always an island path to follow -
its destination uncertain,
but its beauty full of life.

Shoot

The gun survived the fire,
lying there cold and grey,
eyeing us like a dead fish.

He was a son without a father,
swallowed by maternal care,
a Jonah with a freedom wish.

The burden launched him -
seeking, stalking, hunting,
the strength to be a son.

His longing sought a purpose.
Drowning, mouthing at the surface,
his lifebelt was his gun.

Surrounded by the tender,
a gun was hard and clear,
like the father that wasn't there.

Slicing, cleaving, spilling blood,
in control, his freedom dulled,
his love became aware.

Grief found its home
roaming in the wilderness,
with wild tenderness.

Ghost Clock

Cynics say there is no-one there
or that it is an echo,
a mezzo hum bouncing
off rocks behind the cottage.

Some of us know
as twilight falls,
you are not afraid,
and turning from the otters,
stepping inside safely,
the voices creep, mellow.
You hear them crowding
in the entrance hall.
laughing and moving furniture
at five in the morning.

You have a sense it's her:
Virginia McKenna, coaching
her army of ghosts;
not the hoards at four that march
behind the cottage,
where no-one walks, not even otters,
a low insistence of Vikings,
lamenting their dead in the rock's curve,
clanging shields with their swords
and chanting their war cry;

a far cry, at two,
from the tinkle of chinking china
and faint laughter floating -
a dinner party of friends
permeating thick walls.

At one, guests can see
Gavin resting by the fire-place
and at three can be seen
the man in white who walks
beneath the bridge.

None of these vibrations
compare with your imagination.
All we need is pine marten pragmatic,
eating his food at eight, oblivious.

Belonging

You know when the moment comes,
when you walk down the path to
sea-pinks nodding against
a stretch of blue sky,
whose emptiness envelopes you
and fills you with its vastness.

You are here and you could just as easily be there.
Nothing can make you fly to the past or the present.
You relax into what is now,
falling into the firmament,
just a sky watching the clouds.

When the distant drums
that call you
become the tapping of the waves;
when the call of the curlew
or the feel of the wind in your hair
become your lullaby,
then you will know that you are home.

Camusfeàrna

So, when it came to nailing down the lid
he spoke into our eyes.
"The path to freedom's here for us,"
he mouthed with eyes shut fast,
"clean the light so you can see
there's nothing to recall."

I saw him wade through waves of grass
and caught my breath as starlight shone
on tilting bones and shards of shells
that lay along the beach.

Waves spewed pearls
and heart beats shone
with silver spume
but his heart died and with the box
locked tight,
his dust remained forever.

The Host

Closed, the island keeps its tales
of Vikings, shepherds,
lighthouse keepers,
ships with sails, whales
and death, living boundless,
with its ghosts -

an unbroken reminder
that the end is nothing but
a host, a constant friend
taking up different guises
as grasses brown,
and swimmers drown.

Smiling, it invites,
hosting a party to entice
you to flowers, petals, trees and ferns,
birds and voles and otters.

You only have to stand and gaze
at the relentless sea
to feel its spray
and know its myths and fairy tales,
to sense the untouchable
mystery of things gone,

and when the greylag geese visit,
you know the thrill of trust,
of memories of kindness,
the irrevocable bond with place and time
and you know the irony of the cycle
of the end that is endless.

Care for the little things.
The island is our host.
With each death comes a new hope
and the island gives a sign
and opens itself -
to anyone who wants to listen.

Bright Water

Pangs of loss run down the valley's spine,
shivering in the river merged with brine.
Waves are waiting, secrets hid there still,
shouts, long gone, evaporating from the hill.

Lingering breeze plays with the sunbeam glints
whispering 'fire-light' over pebble tints.
Memories, urgent seeping from the sand,
speaking of a man with otters in his hand.

Echoing from the rocks without a sound.
otter hearts forever to us bound.
Spirit sleeping under starry night,
guarding safe a ring of water, bright.

The Present

In the light,
I caught a bird last night.
"He's just right for you.
He'll soon be dead," they said.
Easily resisting all their attempts at rescue,
the collared dove, frightened, hopped
and flustered its way away from them and stopped -
its passage by the dark corner blocked.
There were no mourners present,
the people disengaged, there was no clue.
Easily it let me hold it and as my arms
encircled its frantic fragile body
and held its tiny head against my chest,
I knew in that instant that this was my dream:
things weren't as they seemed.
This was my lame affection,
my present
that will suffice
for me
to rescue
me.

Island Dusk

A blood blonde carnelian.
A lazy iron ocean,
lapping molten in its drowsing,
drops down orange treasure.

Sea shaman slide seamlessly
into brimstone ripples,
spreading silent spells,
plunging impenetrable depths,
diving and surfacing,
parting the metal cauldron,
pulling out the last necklace
of golden amber,
seeping, bleeding,
into the belly of his hunger.

Contextual Notes

When you pass through the wooden gate in the high wall on Eilean Bàn it is like stepping into Hodgson Burnett's 'Secret Garden'. The sense of enchantment is heightened for many people by the reasons that take them there. The way is lined by silver birch and rowan trees, lending the path an air of secret darkness. Voles flit in front of your feet and birds greet you before the shade breaks open to a bright glorious view down Loch Alsh.

The four-acre island has a lighthouse, a lighthouse keepers' cottage, a bothy and bird hide. Part of the lighthouse keepers' cottage is now a holiday let. Gavin's living room was carefully restored by Virginia McKenna and helpers. It became a museum that can be visited in the summer season via an island tour. The end of the cottage has a bed-sit for the volunteer wardens. Being a warden consists of working in the Bright Water Visitor Centre and giving tours of the island. It introduces you to people who visit from all over the world, bringing tales of their memories of Gavin. Children often visit to carry out school projects. The tranquillity and isolation of the island gives opportunities for meditation, writing, painting, and connecting with the colours, textures and peace of nature.

Living on the island as warden for the Bright Water Trust for eight to nine months over the course of three years, gave a seasonal rhythm to observing nature. Each morning the sun rose in dramatic colours, the clouds morphing with sea and mountains. Otters were constant visitors and there was much to see in the area - seals, porpoises and sea eagles. Stags roared nearby when the hillsides turned umber. Sometimes a few eider ducks lazily floated by, or greylag geese flew overhead, reminiscent of Gavin's eider duck enterprise or the greylag geese that he called down to him from the skies, on the beach at Camusfeàrna.

The ever-changing weather brought the ghostly still silence of sea haars and roaring winds that rattled the cottage at night, with storms that landed Manx Shearwaters disrupted in their flights. Rainbows frequently arced the island. When the wind turned chill and changed direction, seagulls wheeled in the currents above the small bluffs at the island's edge. Birds nested on the island and watching the courtship of a pair of oyster catchers was akin to reading a romantic novel as they sat together for a fortnight gazing down the loch.

Common seals favoured the collection of skerries lying just to the north of the island. The low-lying rocks in the water make perfect basking spots, especially for the females expecting young. Towards the end of June, they give birth and make good mothers. The seagulls loiter, making efficient refuse collectors as they pull and fight amongst each other for the after births strewn across the rocks.

As regular as clockwork, in the fading twilight of each evening, there was comfort in the regularity of the trawlers returning to harbour in Kyleakin, followed by a flock of seagulls.

On cloudy nights, with no streetlights on the bridge or island, the darkness could be extreme. In cold weather the sea looks black and syrupy. Pine martens might venture out to tuck into titbits of apple and eggs. On other occasions the Harvest Moon sits huge and gold on the mountaintops, lighting the paths of the island. There's a long tradition of music in the Highlands and memories of the heart-warming harmony of local people singing old traditional songs at ceilidhs, like the sound of a breeze blowing over the muir, gave cheer to the pitch-dark return walks to the cottage.

The neighbouring Isle of Skye is a beautiful island and visiting places such as the nearby Fairy Pools in Glen Brittle, in the shadows of the Cuillin mountains, was once a mysterious and magical affair. Now a famous beauty spot for tourists, the sense of isolation has long gone but the drama of the rocks and the turquoise, ice water is ever present.

Along the road to Elgol, on the Isle of Skye, sits a derelict ancient church and war cemetery at Kilbride. The sheep graze beneath the silent gaze of the mountains and the mists sit long above the moist ground. Faint sounds arise from the reeds and bushes; such as the quiet call of a common snipe, creating evocative sounds of loss and longing.

A short boat ride from Elgol is the Isle of Soay, once home to Gavin Maxwell and his basking shark fishing business. After the Second World War, Gavin was motivated to help the small population on the island and to earn a living for himself with the hunting and fishing skills he had developed on the lands of aristocratic friends and family. Basking sharks were hunted for their oil which was put to a variety of uses – a lubricant for industry, lamps, tonics and food. Gavin wrote about his insight into the contradictions in his relationship with nature and there came a time when he vowed never to hunt again, except for food.

Gavin's passion for nature and caring for wildlife started as a child and showed itself in his unusual ability to connect and bond with wild animals. Later in life, when watching his otters, he experienced a reunion with nature. He never forgot that they were wild animals and sought to provide an environment for them that was free. His life with otters was part of a growing awareness of the fragility of nature and the need for conservation, writing as he did at a similar time to the work of Joy Adamson with her lions and Jane Goodall with the chimpanzees. He urged us, prophetically, to have empathy with animals, to have a reunion with nature, and noted, even then that the writing was on the wall for earth.

Returning to Eilean Bàn from Skye lies over the Skye Bridge, which has been built since Gavin Maxwell lived on the island. It connects the island to the mainland and to the Isle of Skye. At least visitors no longer have to sail out to the island but the bridge brings development and all that the legacy of development entails. The bridge is also sadly, a silent witness to occasional tragedies. Once in a while, drownings occur in the Kyle and sometimes relatives attach, soon to be removed, tiny heart shaped locks to the railings of the Skye Bridge, leaving poignant reminders and heartfelt messages of their love.

Through all the experiences and observations on the island, runs the thread of Gavin and his life. The magic of Eilean Bàn is felt by most people who visit, and you cannot resist its pull and call to nature.

A Spoondrift
of Pearls

Lesley Kahney

A SPOONDRIFT OF PEARLS

Lesley Kahney

POETRY / Subjects & Themes / Nature

PB £7.99 9781528982788

EB £3.50 9781528982795

This lyrical collection of poems is inspired by the tiny island of
Eilean Bàn, lying off the Isle of Skye, the final home to Gavin
Maxwell, author of *Ring of Bright Water*.

Lesley Kahney worked as a volunteer warden on the island for
many months, observing the otters, seals and dolphins; absorbing
the rhythms of the sea, clouds and nature.

Vivid and rich in description, the poems capture the detail in
nature. We catch glimpses of a vanishing Scotland with bothies,
otters and selkies. Using metaphor, symbolism, and mythology,
her poems connect with the history and mystery of the island.
Whether depicting seagulls, primroses or seals; the themes of life,
death, hope, and impermanence linger at the heart of the poems.
With language that is both tender and raw, an emotional journey
is taken through the ordinary and gilded with the microscope of
the extraordinary. Here is an invitation to immerse yourself in the
scent of sea mists and bluebells, and to give your attention in
every moment to being part of nature. Whether a fan of Gavin
Maxwell or not, these poems will speak to anyone who likes
nature or to be by the sea.

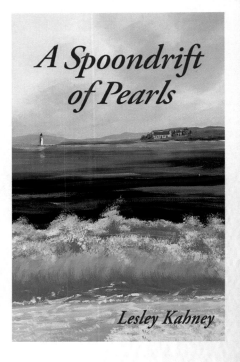

Please send me ...... copy/ies of

A Spoondrift of Pearls
Lesley Kahney

Please add the following postage per book:
United Kingdom £3.00 / Europe £7.50 /
Rest of World £12.00

Delivery and Payment Details

Format	Price	Qty	Total
Paperback ☐			
Subtotal			
Postage			
Total			

Full name: ....

Street Address ....

City:.. County:...

Postcode: .... Country: ....

Phone number (inc. area code): .... Email: ....

I enclose a cheque for £................... payable to Austin Macauley Publishers LTD.

Please send to: Austin Macauley, CGC-33-01, 25 Canada Square, Canary Wharf, London, E14 5LQ

Tel: +44 (0) 207 038 8212
Fax: +44 (0) 207 038 8100
orders@austinmacauley.com
www.austinmacauley.com

AUSTIN MACAULEY PUBLISHERS™
LONDON · CAMBRIDGE · NEW YORK · SHARJAH